The Ministry of Sex

By
GT

M.O.R.E. Publishers
St. Louis, MO

The Ministry of Sex
By
GT

For speaking engagements, poetry recitals, seminars, and conference workshops, e-mail G. T. at:
niflay@yahoo.com

M.O.R.E. Publishers Corp.
P.O. Box 38285
St. Louis, MO 63138

E-mail: MOREPublishersCO@AOL.com
Web: http://www.MOREPublishers.biz

Printed in the United States

The Dedication

For You…
You know, there are so many people who I can
dedicate this to, such as
my Mississippi families, Tennessee friends, and my
little roaming, Air Force buddy. I would like to
thank all of you for your prayers,
efforts and support, but
I have to save my dedications for the One and only
God/Jesus [J.C. ;-)]
Thanks for being there, caring, and keeping me safe,
especially when others and I, couldn't and didn't.
You're truly everything to me!
143,
GT

Preface/Prologue

Loving truth [speaking it, walking in it] and loving sex [talking about it, engaging in it] are two characteristics about me that I hope and pray that God never allow to diminish. I believe in putting it out there and that's exactly what I am attempting to do in this conversation that I'm about to have with you. This won't be your typical novel—which is good because typical is not my goal. I want to be free to talk in the same manner as when conversing with others on a daily basis— not worrying about formatting my sentences just right or being grammatically and politically correct.

My love for truth must've been instilled in me during my time in the womb, or during the very early years of my existence. I've been told that, every since childhood, I've always had a big mouth and spoke what I felt—in good taste, of course, once I learned how to handle the big mouth that I was given. My outspokenness works for me. I am content with being this way because, at least, you know what I am feeling and you don't have to wonder if I'm lying to you. Honesty and truthfulness are critical attributes that should always be included in the making of a good friend.

I've found it a little difficult in today's society to find at least one good friend. People are so deceptive, self-serving, and selfish. They want one-sided relationships—where they do more of the receiving than the giving. They want you to comply with and be flexible to their needs, wants, and desires, but are not willing to put forth that same ideology when it comes down to their mate or friend. Even though these types of people seem to be as numerous as grains of sand, I'm certain that there are still some good, honest, and trustworthy people in our midst.

Now, my affinity for sex, I'm really not sure what brought that on and caused that appetite to be so healthy. Well, you know what, I think it has to do with the fact that I come from sensuous families. In my opinion, they appreciated the act of sex as well as I. My mother's parents had fourteen children and my father's parents had ten or more. Though they seemed to enjoy sex so, back in their child bearing days, they were not as open minded about sex as we are today. Condoms had to have been a foreign concept to them because procreation seemed to happen quite often, and maybe at that point in time the men got more enjoyment out of the sex than the women. The women were more focused on pleasing their husbands than giving attention to their own sexual needs and satisfaction, but things are different now. We are living in a different generation now where sex, at least the basics of it, needs to be discussed because of the alarming rates of diseases and viruses (HIV/AIDS), teenage pregnancy, the wide variety of sexual perversions and other sexual issues that occur in today's society.

Once I put forth the effort to write a book, the topic of sex was definitely not my first choice. When I spoke of my plans to others, the first thing that they would ask was "Is it going to be about sex?"

Initially, I got a little offended because I was like, "I do know how to talk about more than sex." I thought they were insinuating that I was nothing more than some little freak or whore. Then I realized that wasn't the case at all. People just wanted to hear about sex. My inspiration for this book came from the "sex education" sessions that I used to have on Sundays after church at my grandparent's house. The word got out about these teaching sessions, and more and more people would show up. Eventually the sessions kind of faded away, but everyone always asked when I was going to resume our sessions. They never hesitated to let me know how much they enjoyed themselves and how excited they were about the new things that they learned.

Before the sessions at my grandparents' house, sex wasn't openly and thoroughly discussed with the people. The sessions instilled a hunger and desire to know the truth and become liberated in sex—not to stay in sexual bondage feeling ashamed of the sexual nature—acting as if the vagina and penis were put here just for excretion sake. I want the truth to be made known.

When I started the sessions I was still an undergraduate in college and working towards my counseling degree. One of the required classes was Human Sexuality. The teacher of the class was a really nice lady, but she seemed kind of standoffish when it came to teaching the course and handling the questions. I figured it was probably because she didn't want to offend anyone. That was and is the problem. Some people need to be offended.

Sex is so non-disclosed and taboo because people seem to be so uncomfortable with it for some reason, or have been made to feel as if it is dirty and unnatural. I mean you don't have to give a run down of all your sexual encounters and tell how far you've gone to please a person. That's not what talking about sex equates to. Some times the tough and difficult issues do have to be tackled simply because there are people who want to know and need to know what really goes on.

Not all of the info that I learned about sex came from college. A great deal of it came from personal experiences and from the Man upstairs (God in Heaven). My stance is this; if someone is seeking truth and if I have it available to give, why keep it to myself?   I'm not about oppressing, belittling, or keeping people in the dark.   Please be enlightened. Please want and strive for more.   Please push yourself to reach your best potential.   Please make every single second of the life that you have count. Life is not a practice run; there's no rewind and re-record option to it.

Who Is G. T. [God's Treasure]?

By GT

Tainted beyond measure, my usual first thought was
pleasure;
Never thinking that I could be one of God's treasures.
Feelings of inadequacy seeped in because of pictures
that were painted by the church folks that I knew.
But just as Jesus loves them, the song says He also
loves me too.
Always being judged and in constant competition
with myself,
sometimes too proud to admit that I need help.
Flashing back on who I was just a short time ago—
I now see how God had plans for me, even when I
was a whore.
Always talking some big talk—
But not always willing to take that walk.
I used to hide in the shadows of helping others
achieve, but
I had to wise up because some had malicious
motives hidden up their sleeves.

Immersing myself in a world filled with lust and sex,
I eventually had to stop because my spirit felt vexed.
Though it seemed good while it lasted,
I knew that I was more than just some warm, wet
cat.
I was put here to share myself with the world,
but in a more productive form than that.
I sometimes smoked weed to relax my mind when
My thoughts were in a whirlwind. I attempted to
convince myself
That it just grew like that, so it shouldn't be a sin.
Listening to the devil caused me to feel weak and
defected,
Dismissing the fact that I was purposely made by my
Creator
for in my weakness is where His strength was and is
perfected.
I've been so mad at times, that the acts I plotted up
would have surely
robbed me of my freedom.
Now I feel inclined to stress the importance of never
allowing someone else to keep you out of the
Kingdom.

It boggles my mind to think that I could be one of the ones that He uses,

but it would be my gracious pleasure to share in the family of those He chooses.

Now that I look through eyes that have a much clearer view,

I see I've fallen short on some things, and now it is time to "make it do what it do."

Perfection is a place that I know I'll never reach,

But I can surely strive for it by practicing every word that I preach.

Haters may attempt to try and tear me down—but their hating tells me that I'm somebody,

so this princess needs her crown.

Tormenting experiences provoke me to put people up on

The real game of life—for I'd love to see lives filled with joy

and peace, not misery and strife.

Almost lost my mind twice, but God said it wasn't no having that,

And after the second time He saved my life,

He commanded me to go get my life back.

So now I'm on a path searching for who GT really
is—
And one of the most reassuring facts is knowing that
I'm His.
I want more and I'm taking the steps to get it.
I'm holding on to the motto that I've got only one
life—so I got to live it.
Dismissing limited ways of thinking is hard but it
will help me find how much I'm worth—
I know I've been destined for greatness every since
my first day on earth.
Thoughts of suicide attempted to corrupt my mind
when I was a pre-teen.
I felt my life was a curse of evil and living good was
just a dream.
At an early age, I found out the hard way that things
were not always as they seemed—
but I know that satan was attempting to kill me
because he knew I was destined to be a queen.
I've wanted to throw in the towel so many times,
But I would hate to miss my blessings and there's no
such thing as pressing rewind.

I know that a winner never quits and a quitter never
wins.

I find consolation in God's love and in His
forgiveness of my sins.

I thank You for loving me, God, even when I don't
do as I should;

and today I strive to walk in purpose and hold on to
the promise that all things work for my good.

The Ministry of Sex

Let's Get Naked

Putting it out There

That's what it's made for

My Sexual Career

Journey into the "Life"

Resolution of the Climax

The Last Drop

Let's Get Naked

Let's talk about something that is over glamorized, while the truth of the matter lies hidden. Let's talk about the one issue that many seem so afraid to address, but everyone wants to and seems to enjoy participating in. Let's talk about the one thing that causes some to take it by force when they are turned down or when it is not willingly offered to them; the thing that produces pedophilic lusts and puts innocent and unsuspecting children in a position to be fondled and molested. Let's talk about what makes us so hedonistic [pleasure driven] that an overwhelming number of individuals disregard the opposite sex and turn to the same sex as they are. Let's talk about the thing that causes some to even go so far as to experiment with animals—all for pleasure and orgasm sake. I mean, let's talk about something that feels so good that we are willing to put our health on the line—even our lives, just because it feels better raw. Something that's a drug within itself, seems to cause addictions beyond measure, and breaks up happy homes—sometimes without remorse. Let's talk about something that makes some forget all sense of morals, values, beliefs, ethics, standards, and etc. all for the sake of experiencing the momentary pleasure to be received. In the famous words of Salt ~N~ Pepa, LET'S TALK ABOUT SEX.

Am I downing sex and making it out to be some kind of life--destroying bandit? By no means is that my goal. I simply want to talk about and tackle the natural phenomenon that is so popular, yet at the same time, so taboo. Why are we so afraid to discuss something that affects us all? I truly believe that if we embraced the subject of sex, then a wide variety of sexual based issues and cases {teenage pregnancy, rape, molestation, STDs, HIV, AIDS, etc.} could be reduced. I'm not saying that all of these things will cease to happen, but what I am saying and do believe is, if curiosities are addressed instead of being left up to the individual to find out on his/her own, the numbers could possibly be significantly reduced. For those seeking statistics, you won't find any here...I'm just conversing, or maybe it's better to call this a monologue. Since not many others seem bold enough or seem to care enough about this issue to address it, then I'm attempting to speak up and do my part to assist my predecessors and help give a voice, an opportunity, and to open a door for those to come.

Putting it out there

You have the right to believe what you want, but I believe the initial discussions about sex must start at home. Please allow me to say that having a real/truthful/enlightening conversation with your child [-ren] does not equate to telling your daughters "if you're going to give it up, at least get paid for it—don't give it away for free". Now, by all means, I do agree that the vagina should not be passed out like a hot commodity—but don't encourage the baby to be a prostitute. The last time that I heard, prostitution is still illegal in the USA—and the only exception is in Vegas—and only if you live there. I still am not encouraging that kind of theology. In regards to sons, telling them to "pimp these hoes" or encouraging them to believe that one of the attributes that makes men real men is having a large number of sexual conquests is not cute nor is it acceptable. I'm almost certain that there are a nice handful of men, who at this very moment, wish they would have kept their "little man" in their pants because if they did, they would not be experiencing the baby momma drama, child support, penicillin shots, crabs, HIV, and whatever else they may be going through.

Also parents, I know that some schools offer sex education—well, at least they did when I was in high school and I recall that it wasn't a very informative lecture. Anyway, those teachers are only allowed to discuss so much, and they don't know your child (ren) as you do. The job is not theirs but yours to tell your child (ren) what he/she/they need to know. We all were young once, so I'm sure you have an overall gist of what questions children have. Instead of labeling them "hot, fast, or mannish" take the initiative to share the info for which they are looking. If you do not, then the children will hear about sex from friends or someone else who may be just as less informed as they are. Children will more than likely be told about how good it is/was, which is a lie, most times; because I've heard so many people say that their first sexual experience was awful. They just did it because they felt that they really liked or were in love with the person they give it up to. Another reason why children engage in sex is because they want to experience what they've heard so much about it. If the information has already been offered to and instilled in them, it's possible that they won't be so easily swayed by peer pressure or the desire to fit in with the in-crowd.

Even if abstinence is what you teach your children, still be open enough with them and give them the truth because in these days and times, abstinence and saving your virginity until marriage seems to be a foreign concept in this country that was founded on Christian principles. If your child (or even you) decides to be celibate, I pray to God for their (your) strength and will--power because it's hard out here for a celibate person, especially when it seems as if everything around you is filled with sex. Trust me; I know first hand since I've rediscovered my virginity. Temptation is always available, and you don't have to ask for it or beckon it to come in your direction.

I know that some say that experience is the best teacher, but some experiences you don't need. It may just be best to take someone else's word because some experiences can turn into regrets. For the parents who simply tell their children "don't have sex because it's wrong or because God will punish you", please don't leave them hanging like that. What if they catch you in the act? Then comes the "I'm a grown man/woman and I can do what I want, you're just a child" or the "do as I say not as I do". Give them more of an explanation than that. Children are a lot smarter and seemingly cleverer these days than for what they are given credit. Those tactics may work for a while, but once they hear how good sex is, that everyone is doing it, that sex was the process by which they were conceived, and that you, the parent engage in sexual activity as well, they will have questions that will demand answers and curiosities that will long to be satisfied. Explain that with sex come responsibilities, connections, and emotions that young bodies, souls and minds are not mature enough as pre-teens and teenagers to handle.

By all means, they do need to be made aware, at least, of the basics because the changes they experience during puberty are in harmony with sex. A natural occurrence for boys is nocturnal emissions, or wet dreams. Do you honestly think they aren't going to wonder why they wake one, or a couple of mornings, with their underwear crusted and sticking to their pubic area? And as for girls, breasts grow, nipples harden, and menstruation happens. Just like me, I'm sure the girls will be curious to know why they bleed every month. The simplest and most honest reason to give is that menstruation happens because no semen/sperm was taken in vaginally to cause conception; therefore, the unfertilized egg is being "thrown away/discarded".

Stop telling "cute fables" and having children looking crazy and falling for anything. It's just so much easier and enlightening to tell the truth—unless, as a parent, you don't know the whole truth either. There is too much going on. Don't play mind games or be dishonest with children, even with people in general, and not just regarding sexual conversations. I'm just saying that once children are of age enough to receive and comprehend the "Birds and the Bees", by all means, love and care about the babies enough to give them genuine truth.

That's what it's made for

A young songwriter has a song on his *Confessions* album entitled "That's What It's Made For". It's a song about sex that, I assume, is supposed to give some rationality to freely passing out the goodies. Now before I go any farther, let me please say that I AM NOT bashing the songwriter— so if you know him, or even if he happens to read these words, I'm illustrating a point. Actually, I have the CD and was very fond of this particular song when I began listening to this CD. That's exactly why I feel as if I can use this song to say what I'm trying to say. I know how some folk are. They will be going back saying, "Gyrl, she was hating on the songwriter. See gyrl, that's what I'm talking about, black folks always trying to hate on the next one—

she just mad 'cause he got more stacks than she does". No, people, that's not what's going on here. The songwriter and everyone else are free to be themselves, just as I am free to be me. So anyway, back to the subject at hand—just had to get that disclaimer out of the way.

In the song, he starts off talking about how he thought he'd just have a one night rendezvous with a young lady, but she just made it so good to him that he had to go back and lay in/with her again. Then it got that much better to him that he got caught up in the vagina and decided to go in raw [no condom]—fully aware that he shouldn't have done that. He even decided that he would free himself within her because it felt too good to pull out. Though I am not a man, I've been in this situation before, engaging in unprotected sex and not wanting the penis to be pulled out, knowing that I should not have allowed those babies to be freed within me. I guess that's why the young songwriter (and I) was "confessing" about a baby being made--all because of "getting lost in the sauce". Thank you Jesus that I had a miscarriage! That's another story that I will have to

30

share later. So in his chorus he says "Go on and hit it, that's what it's made for/ We got protection, that's what it's made for/ Boo why you trippin'? You know I got it/ That's what it's made for". Even though I liked the song, I have to disagree with him. Our selfish, hedonistic lusts would have us to believe that this example is what sex was made for, but sorry hun, that's not it.

Although we're just chatting, I delight in the truth—giving it and receiving it, so I plan on giving the truth whether it's wanted or not. Now, even if you don't believe in God, the initial purpose of sex will more than likely apply to you and is still very relevant. So here we go. Sex's initial purpose is to be the act that actually consummates the marriage. That's why some wait until the wedding night to indulge—and even for those who didn't wait, did it feel better to you and did you feel more free to do all those kinky, freaky, and nasty thoughts and fantasies that you had in mind after you were married?

You see, God ordained marriage as the earthly/physical covenant relationship to mirror His covenant/promise with the church/body of Christ. So because there is liberation in God, through Christ, for this reason, He says that the marriage bed is undefiled – meaning you are free to get as freaky as you want – as long as the covenant is not violated. Therefore, sex in this perspective is seen as the most intimate form of contact, I'll even go so far to say that it's similar to the act of worship.

Worshipping God and spending time in His presence are the most intimate forms of contact that we have with Him. When we lay in His presence, we express our deepest love and desire for Him, and spend our own personal time with Him [no one else can worship for you – it's just you and God, no third, fourth or fifth party] as an effort to become more closely united with Him. Worship music and songs were created to assist us in getting to that intimate and holy place with Him – not that we need it, but this form of music just helps to usher us into His presence. More than likely, this is why; worship music is slow, intimate, and passionate – like a love song to the Father.

If marriage is the relationship ordained to mirror this, then sex with your spouse should be the most intimate, most intense, most fulfilling, most pleasurable, and most self-sacrificing method of expressing your affinity. Your desire to please the one you're in covenant with should be greater than the few or many that you had before your spouse. Sex, in this union, should be the most liberating sex, and should show your desire, love, and affinity for your mate. Just as with worship music, this is why Luther Vandross, the Isley's, Marvin Gaye, and so many others were blessed with the precious gifts of writing love songs and ballads to help coax the passion and heighten the love sessions. I mean, I know that you don't need music to enhance your sexual performance, but if you did choose some background music, who would want gospel songs like, Donnie McClurkin's "We Fall Down"? That just wouldn't work for me.

Referencing the previous paragraph, in the relationship with God, no outside person can assist you in the pure intimate worship you give to God. Therefore, in a matrimonial relationship, a group session [ménage –a--trois] is not going to enhance your marriage. It will just make things more complicated. You wouldn't be able to get lost in each other because you have another participant to focus on. Though it may feel physically pleasing, it doesn't connect you and your spouse together spiritually, as it would if it was just the two of you.

As I mentioned about worship earlier, one of the greatest experiences derived from worship is getting lost in the Spirit of and presence of God; losing all sense of self, surroundings, and time. Getting so caught up that once coming out, you may feel drained, lifted, intoxicated, and etc, but definitely feeling closer and more connected to Him. Well, let's think about sex for a minute [between a man and woman]. Let's visualize one of the ways that we can comprehend feeling closer to, obtaining a deeper connection with, and achieving "oneness" with our spouse. Sex is the one thing that truly connects the two.

Once the penis is inserted into the vagina, it can no longer be seen unless it's pulled out. The vagina provides a suction effect to pull the penis inside and a tightening/gripping effect to keep it inside. Both partners find a rhythm of their own and

34

each stroke/thrust creates a harmony, both attempting to give the other more pleasure than they are receiving. With some, they become so in sync that they both reach orgasm together and if/when he ejaculates within her, reproduction happens; bringing forth life, created out of the two unifying as one; a baby being the result of the "oneness". It becomes the physical example we are all able to take in of two people joining together as one flesh. He/she has characteristics and traits of both parents but is a single entity. So, sex was always meant to be life-giving, never to be life-threatening and life-destroying as it is today.

And for us single people, God already knew beforehand that, although He laid out the law that pre-marital sex was not what we were supposed to be doing with ourselves, some of us would not be able to sustain our lusts until marriage. That is why He sent that message through apostle Paul [those of you who read your Bible or go to church should know him]. He said he would rather that you be single, keep your genitals to yourself, and commit yourself to be more effective for God; but for those of us who couldn't control our lusts – it is better for us to be married and be free to be freaks in the right relationship than to keep passing out the sex to any and everybody, going against God's wishes each and every time we commit. Also, think about this; if sex is used to consummate marriage, then to how many people are you married? Sex is intimate and connects you to the person with whom you are having sex. So, if you're sexing somebody crazy, then they've signed their autograph on you and left a little gift to remember them by in your spirit. I've had my share of crazies. I guess that's why I have all kinds of issues and can't always think straight. I've had my dozens of partners and share of one-niters, and I promise you that I could not and still cannot see myself spending a few days, months, or years with the majority of them—so I would be a miserable sistah if I had to spend the rest of my life with them.

At some point, I had to come to the conclusion that my "little girl" (vagina) was such a small portion of who I was and am, so I needed to gain some control over her and stop allowing her to lead this body of mine – especially into situations that

I would have otherwise not been in, had it not been for me letting the little girl guide me. Honestly, I do miss the pleasure that I derived from sex and look forward to receiving it again. At this point I realize that EVERYONE is not capable of and/or worthy enough to receive the goodness that I have to offer. So it's just best that I keep it tight for now. Also, it's not that I haven't been tempted to engage in sex, I just know what I want. I am trying hard not to settle for anything less, and I'm capable of focusing on more important things than momentary pleasure and temporary fixes. I've had some great escapades, but I'm ready for the intensity, intimacy, and freedom to be, in the words of Luke and 2 Live Crew, "as nasty as I want to be" and truly enjoy the "greatest sex" that R. Kelly sang about. At this point, I feel that marriage is the only way for me to obtain that because "that is what it was made for".

MY SEXUAL CAREER

Out of all the many things that the various people who are or have been in and out of my life could choose to say about me, I think there are at least two things that they all may have jotted down, in agreement, on a list. One is that I've always been a lover of truth and realness; and two, that I have always appreciated sex, especially the good kind. I pray to God that my love for truth never diminishes and while I'm walking in the truth and tossing up a prayer, I may as well go ahead and say that I don't really want Him to take away my appreciation for sex either. What I do pray is that He links me up with a good man who can appreciate the same.

In regards to my sexual career, it started a little earlier than I would have wanted. I can recall the days of my childhood when I was cajoled into performing sexual acts on a male who was at least nine to ten years my senior. That was something that I never really shared with anyone because I trusted the man, just as you would trust a harmless family member. I thought that all was well because he wasn't violating me; at least that's how I saw it then. Regardless to whether I was pleasuring him or he was fondling me—as a child it was wrong. I think that as I got older, I repressed the thoughts because once I became aware of what was really going on, I was disgusted and vowed, to myself, to never really speak of it nor remember those moments again. But once you start dissecting yourself and wondering why you are the person you are, why you have certain behavior traits and act the way you do most times, you will find that the things that happened during your first few years on this earth, shape the adult you grow up to be. As young adults, going through the phase of finding ourselves, usually in the mid to late twenties and early thirties, we spend time peeling off layers of who we were taught or forced to be, what we were made to believe of ourselves (be it positive or negative), and the many opinions that others had/have of us, all in an effort to find out who we really are and how we define ourselves—not based on any outside factors. Going through the period of finding yourself is usually difficult for most because there are so many things that you have to face and deal with that you thought would never resurface again. I guess that's why when you go to visit a therapist, to get to core/root of the reason for your visit, childhood is an intricate period that is always visited.

Mirroring the pattern of a lot of youth, I heard about the pleasures and experiences of sex through friends and cousins who were in my same age group—with some starting to engage in sexual intercourse during their pre-teens. Hearing the things that I heard, of course, piqued my interest and got my thoughts flowing, wondering what would take place when I did engage in sex? With whom would I do it? How would it feel once I did do it?

I began having consensual intercourse when I was sixteen (meaning, there was a moment when I engaged in sex that I did not willingly want to engage in—though I did share this with some, no one really took me seriously because I knew the person, so this was another incident that I just kept to myself). By this time, I wanted to experience all that I knew about sex on my first attempt. I wanted to experience the acts that I saw performed on the porn that I snuck and watched; and I wanted to experience the oral pleasure that my older friends spoke about. Though I didn't know it at the time, killing cats would become my specialty because my sexual curiosity would end up leading me down paths that I may have otherwise not traveled had I not been led by lust. So, needless to say, on my first sexual encounter, I did all that my mind imagined, even though I wasn't completely sure of and aware of how to do it and wasn't exactly sure what pleasure I was supposed to derive from it. All I knew was that I heard it was good, so I figured I'd try. Not that I was being a follower, but I wanted some pleasure for a change because I spent so much time trying to please others that I seemed to have lost myself in the process. Though I wasn't seeking to find my confidence through sex [I've always thought that was shallow], my wanting to engage in a hobby or activity that was pleasing to me and about my satisfaction was not justifiable reasoning either. Because this satisfaction was only temporary, my desires grew and my mind started to become more open to all the possibilities for enjoyment to be derived from the three letters, S.E.X.

With my first, I figured that after him, I wouldn't have sex again until I got married, but I haven't had sex with him in almost ten years and I'm definitely not married—so I can admit that I told one of the biggest lies the day that I made that statement. At that time, that was really what I thought, but again I say, desires grew and my mind changed. It wasn't until my third partner that I realized the apex of pleasure to be obtained through sex: the Orgasm. It happened so fast, but it felt so good and didn't last long enough, but if it did last any longer, I don't think that I would have been able to handle it. At that point, I was like "oh, this is what I'm supposed to be getting from this". With that being said, that is one of the main reasons why kids should not be having sex because they don't even understand what's really happening. It took me about two or three years before I ever experienced those seconds of pleasure.

Beforehand, I was just assisting in producing pleasure for the dudes.

Receiving cunnilingus was one thing that I grew to appreciate and became accustomed to. I enjoyed engaging in fellatio as well, but I knew that putting my mouth on every Tom, Dick, and Harry was not what needed to be going down. With each partner, my imagination grew more and more vivid and my desires became more intense. Hedonistic behavior really started to settle in, and if I didn't receive the pleasure that I was seeking, then it was no need for any guy that I was sexing to expect another chance. I know and believe that when you're out there having sex with a collective mix of people, everyone you encounter is not going to be pleasing to you. Some will perform better than others, some will be bigger/smaller than others, some will go longer/shorter than others, etc. Though some say that this is a way of "test driving the car before you buy it" and is a good way of finding out what you like/don't like, that may be a personal truth for somebody, but I think this leaves too much room for unnecessary comparison. Would you miss out on your soul mate because he or she didn't sex you as good as someone you may have had before? If you didn't have anyone else to compare him/her to, how would you know if he/she was bad in bed? But like me, so many others have engaged in pre-marital sex, so may I offer a suggestion to us all? Let us not marry for the sex. Personally, I would want to marry someone with whom I've never had sex with simply because sex wouldn't be a determining factor in the growth or decline of our relationship. Building a relationship based on good sex is not going to last anyway. What if, at some point, your mate couldn't perform sexually? What if the sexual attraction declines? Then what form of attraction is left? What if your mate becomes paralyzed from the waist down? Some may say that as long as from the waist up everything is still working then they're good...well, hypothetically speaking, what if the mate becomes paralyzed from the neck down? Seek more in a relationship than just a good sex buddy.

Okay, now back to what I was saying before that tangent. My lusts grew hungrier and I wanted to feed them. Almost every sexual fantasy that I had, I made arrangements to carry out. Group sessions, various positions, filling various orifices, voyeurism, exhibitionism, the list goes on. But there came a time during my "career" that I was presented a "temporary assignment" that I was reluctant to go on, but despite my hesitance, I obliged. I "worked" willingly for about three and a half to four years; but please believe that once I quit, I planned to never take that "job/position" again.

A DEAD END LOVE

BY GT

A smile spreads across my face as I reminisce

On moments of joy and happiness--

Remembering all the pleasure you gave,

And how much, for your love, I craved.

I felt like your queen and we ruled the world

together,

Seemed like you were the best at all you did

And no one could do it better.

Being with you had me feeling like I was on top of

the world,

You helped me find the woman in me and to say bye-

bye to the little girl.

Anything that I asked for, you put forth your best

effort to get.

You loved the way that I loved you back and didn't
mind showing it.
Every thing just felt so good that I got caught up in
A love affair that was never supposed to be--
Not realizing that I was in bondage,
Walking around thinking that I was free.
There came a day when my fairy tale world came to a
shattering end.
I then realized that my so-called lover was my enemy
Disguised as a friend.
You already had thousands of lovers, but that just
wasn't enough!
You wanted to spread yourself around to see
how many more you could corrupt.
If only I would have listened to my true Friend and
Not fell prey to you in the first place,
I would not have been thinking with my lusts,
Ignoring the obvious warning signs right before my
face.
You were so clever and manipulative at the way you
spit that game,
Only to soon leave your lovers in a pool of misery
and shame.

So many are so wrapped around your finger

That they never want to leave you,

Knowing that they are living a lie,

But are insanely trying to make it the truth.

I would think that by now, some of them would have

wised up,

And stop turning blind eyes to the fact that

You've infected so many and left them lying in the

dust.

I had to wise up because I was headed no where fast,

Investing myself in a relationship that I knew

wouldn't last.

I realized that I meant nothing to you, but like a fool,

I cried when I left you alone –

I blame myself for that because I knew it was wrong

all along.

It's been an uphill journey and I've gotten myself on

track,

So I bid you farewell homosexuality, I ain't ever

coming back.

Journey into "the Life"

Reflecting on this period in my life, I really have to say that if I had a chance to go back and choose a sin to commit; this would not be one of them. I mean, I feel as if I've always been "gay-friendly" and held to the philosophy, that your business is truly your own business and it's your own accountability about who you choose to sleep with, just don't try to coerce me into it. Yes, Jesus, I know that I am a little on the freaky/kinky/open-minded side, but that was just more than what I planned on getting myself involved. Despite whether or not I would have willingly chosen to partake in this, I did end up on the journey.

This chapter of my life was like a birthing process. A) The seed had to be planted, B) the water had to break, and C) the baby had to be born. So shall we begin with the "seed planting" stage?

A)   It started back about ten or eleven years ago when I was working at a large retail store. I remember that there was a guy there who worked in the customer service department. My initial reaction when I first saw him was that he was a homosexual [← from this point on, I may use the word "homie" to interchangeably define this term]. I arrived at this conclusion because of purple contacts he used to wear, the sassy attitude that he had, the feminine features/characteristics/qualities that he had, and a few other things that raised rainbow colored flags. Not to say that I was right in automatically making a judgment call about this brotha whom I didn't even know, but I just was accustomed to rough, rugged, country men from Mississippi who were nothing like this guy. Because I didn't want to judge a book by its cover, I really wanted to and tried to give him the benefit of the doubt. I mean, he did have a girlfriend who was carrying his baby at the time. Of course that didn't mean anything, but at that time, I didn't know anything about being on the down low, heck I barely knew anything about homosexuals. So time went on and we worked together for a year or so before we actually got to know each other. What kind of broke the ice between us was singing. I was singing to myself at work one day and he overheard me. So he was like "you sound good". So I thanked him and I think I asked if he could sing or not? I don't recall if he said yeah or nay, but I do recall him singing—and why did he do that? After that moment, I gave him my number and told him that he needed to call me and sing me to sleep.

We talked over the phone and I got to know him a little better and figured that he was a pretty cool dude for the most part. We began hanging outside of work with a mutual friend of ours, and probably about a year later, we ended up having sex [he was the first but was not the last homie that I had sex with]. Please allow me to interject to bring up something in the previous chapter. Having sex connects you and creates soul ties between you and your partner. So because I didn't have this knowledge before hand, I didn't know what all I was getting myself into at that time. Though we only had sex a few times, each time felt better than the last— but for some reason, a little voice within me still questioned his sexuality. On several occasions, I'd ask if he was a homie, and he would always respond with cussing and "hell naw", asking why I kept asking that question and telling me not to ask anymore. For a while, I honored his request, but I still couldn't quiet the voice within [this is why I now live by the phrase "you know the truth by the way it feels"]. The mutual friend we had was very involved in our little "situation" and there would be times when I would ask him about Mr. Purple Eyes' sexuality, but I never got much of an answer from him. What I did notice about the mutual friend was that he seemed to be unenthused each and every time that Purple Eyes and I would engage in any form of affection and sex—almost as if he was jealous [later to find out that it was the latter because they were having sex during the same time that he and I were sexing]. He too gave me the impression that underneath the overly expressed interest in females, he preferred men. Whenever I would ask him about his sexual preference, he would respond by saying that I hurt his feelings—what kind of mess is that? With that response alone, my questions were answered. Within this clique, was a third party, a minister, who also set my "gaydar" off. The mutual friend and Purple Eyes were both members of the minister's community choir. So, I was thinking, surely if he is a minister, he can't be a homie too. That wouldn't be a cute thing to do. One thing I don't believe in doing is playing church and playing with God. I'm not saying that the minister, or any of the guys [they all had a love for "church"] didn't love or know God, but my thing is how can you teach/preach to me the truth when you are living a lie? That's just contradictory and those two things just don't go together. I'm sure that we have all done some things that we knew were not right, but we shouldn't expect others to follow our directions or take our advice as the truth when we are not leading by example.

One day, after choir rehearsal, the minister suggested that we go to this club/bar that he wanted us to check out. He told us beforehand that it was a gay club and acted pretty appalled by the idea of a club of this nature existing, when he was the one who set up the field trip. So everyone, some more willingly than others, agreed to tag along. Once we got there, I was more appalled than any of them. It was a predominantly black male gay bar and it really hurt my feelings to see those men groping, kissing, grinding on, and fondling with each other. One thing that I remember the mutual friend of me and Mr. Purple Eyes saying was that a place like that would bring the true nature out of a man [woman]; and with that being said, I was expecting some revelation.

After my second or third visit to the club, I gave up going because it was just too overwhelming for me, but as for the guys, they went religiously, every weekend—Fridays, Saturdays, and I think they may have went on Sundays as well. Um, quick question, what heterosexual man would be in gay club three days a week, every week, for years and still sing the song that he is not gay? I knew then that my speculations couldn't have been too biased-- seemed like I was speaking the truth instead of passing judgment.

The time that I spent with those friends decreased drastically, and whenever I would suggest that we hang out together, they would always retort with "you know where we be so if you want to hang then you got to come to our spot". Usually I would say "I'm good, maybe some other time". During that same time, I had a homegyrl who loved to go to the gay club and watch the drag show, and, a few times, I let her talk me into going. I didn't care for the show, but I loved to dance. After the show was over, I would get my dance on for a minute and then we would dip out.

On one of those occasions that we went out, I met a guy. It was obvious that I wasn't what he was attracted to and neither was I attracted to him. He was noticeably tipsy, but he was a nice guy and we enjoyed ourselves, chatting the night away. During our chat session, he proceeded to tell me about his "husband" whom he felt was cheating on him. He talked about how much he loved and cared for the dude, but really felt like the guy was not being faithful to him. Though I didn't really care for or condone the lifestyle, he was still a human being that deserved to be listened to and given attention and respect. So I tried to console him as best as I could and he seemed to be appreciative of my efforts. The music was blaring loud, so instead of shouting words over the music, we just went ahead and decided to end the conversation. He gave me a hug and told me that he loved me; I hugged him back and thought nothing else of the conversation.

I danced on and maybe thirty minutes to an hour later, my little friend came back and tapped me on my shoulder. Shouting over the music, he told me that he wanted me to meet his husband, and I complied. I was standing there trying to figure out how this introduction was going to go because, up until thirty or more minutes prior, I had no clue of who this young man was, nor did I figure I would know his "husband". He walked up, and the other man's hand that he was holding when he introduced me was none other than Mr. Purple Eyes. I really had to gain some composure quickly because my adrenaline started pumping and, at that moment, I could have opened up an enormous "can of whoop a—", and seriously whipped some "tale". I pushed back my anger, smiled and said, "Hey husband, you sure do look familiar". I may have been in that club five or ten minutes longer and then I couldn't take it anymore. I told homegyrl to come on and we got on down. On the ride home, I thought about the many times that I asked questions and got cussed out badly. I recounted the times that I overlooked and disregarded the truth within me because I wanted to give him the benefit of the doubt. Most of all, I thought about the two or three times that we had unprotected sex. Mad and disgusted, I couldn't blame anyone but myself because I knew the truth, but for some reason, I chose not to listen to it. This is one of the few, of many, things to get caught up in when being led by your genitals.

For a while, afterwards, I didn't talk to Mr. Purple Eyes or anyone else in their clique for that matter. I took my hiatus because, all along, they all knew what was going on and the more that I asked them, the more they lied to me and tried to make me seem like I was wrong for my speculations. Time passed and I got over it because I try hard to not hold grudges.

After dealing with those shenanigans, I was really looking to Jesus for some assistance. I guess at this point, we were all kind of getting on the same page [at least that's what I thought]. The clique didn't frequent the club scene as often, possibly not at all, and decided that they'd give a little more time to Jesus as well. Instead of weekends filled with bar hopping, "churchin'" became the replacement. It seemed like there were more than enough community choirs in Memphis for each one of them to have an event almost every Saturday or Sunday evening. I went with the clique to the programs from time to time because it was something to do on the weekend, but what and who I saw at the church functions were not much different from what I experienced at the gay club.

There was a time when I do remember attending one service that had a choir there that stood out more to me than the rest. They seemed a little different, maybe a little more genuine even. This was

60

one of those professional choirs who had several gospel albums recorded and their songs were in rotation on the gospel stations, locally and nationally. I figured that this would be a good way to help me get focused and give more of my self and my time to Jesus and use, at least, one of the gifts/talents that God gave me. I did not know that this would lead to the "water breaking/dilation phase" of my "pregnancy".

B) I really had no idea of the "world" that I was getting myself into when I got involved with these "church folks". How many know that there is a difference between "church folk" and a Christian truly seeking the Word with a sincere heart? If you haven't had that rude awakening yet, then let me please advise you that there is a difference. Now, I'm not saying that not any of those people were truly seeking Jesus and salvation because I don't know what kind of relationship anyone else has with God— I just know about mine. We all do our share of dirt and commit our share of sins, but if you're going to church—especially if you're actively involved in ministry, there are some changes that need to and will take place. If you truly repent and ask for forgiveness, deliverance, and whatever else you need God to do, asking with sincerity, it's clearly stated throughout the Bible, that He will give you what you need. So, if you're comfortably practicing sins and are not trying to change, that is not what's up, but I respect your decision. Believe me, I do know first hand, if you say you know Him and continue to go against His will, He will handle you—and His punishment, I really don't think you would want that because it is no fun at all. We all will truly reap what we sow—that's not a cute cliché, but it's real talk. His punishment can really be miserable; and despite the fact that I experienced the wrath of punishment, I thank Him for allowing me to go through it on the front end while I am still young. I prefer for it to have happened that way than coming back to haunt me when I get older—good looking out Jesus!

When I first got involved with the choir, I really had a passion in my heart to sing and grow spiritually. I just knew this was going to assist me in my spiritual elevation, and it did, just not in the way that I thought. The people seemed to be pretty cool and it seemed like a good fit for me. So I contributed my time and efforts to the choir, being a faithful member and attempted to form some good and productive relationships with the people. Then one day, I guess the charade was over and the fake masks came off. Some of those people had the worst attitudes I had ever encountered. The choir was very cliquey, some of the women were too catty, one person was sleeping with another person's spouse, all kinds of tension and animosity, and I could just go on. One day, during a studio session, a fight broke out or was very close to breaking out and I just had to ask everyone, "Are we not doing this for Jesus? Isn't this supposed to be ministry?" Everybody just kind of stood there looking at me crazy and seemingly in disbelief and disgust that I asked such an "outlandish" question. After the looking party was over, everyone just kind of resumed their conversations and activities, but there was one lady who pulled me to the side and said to me "I understand what you were asking, but you have to remember that you are dealing with flesh". I just said okay and continued on with the recording session.

Now, I'm not claiming to be perfect, and my flesh has gotten the best of me on several occasions, but I just don't take ministry or any work for the Lord as a joke or just something to do—especially when other people's souls/spirits are involved. I try to stay on God's good side as much as I can because I've experienced punishment from Him on several occasions and do not want to go through those "hell on earth" experiences again. Recalling those experiences makes it's easier for me to get myself together and put forth my best effort to keep Him satisfied with GT.

Eventually, my participation with the choir dwindled, but I was still involved with a majority of the people because a nice portion of the choir members went to the same church that I was attending. It was a rather small church, mostly choir members and the pastor's family [who, by the way was the leader/founder of the choir]. Sunday after Sunday and Wednesday after Wednesday I would faithfully attend the services, lifting my hands in praise to God and shedding tears in my time of worship. Often times, the services involved the laying on of hands, speaking in tongues, and anointing with oil. By all means, I was and am for this type of service. The sad thing is that you really have to be cautious at church because the spirits that are leading the services may cause you more problems than you had before you went to the service. Week after week, I would go down for altar call and the ministers, elders, and pastor would lay hands on pretty much everyone who came to the altar to cast their cares on Jesus.

I can recall inviting people to church with me, but usually they would say no or make comments like "you go to that gay church". I would get defensive, thinking that, surely, most of these people are not gay. Well, I end up finding out that those people were right. The majority of the ministry leaders were homosexuals—and those were the ones laying hands and praying over the members. You see, here's my issue with that; when we go to a church service, we go with open hearts, minds, and spirits, open to receive God and His Word. And it is often said that the spirit of the leader trickles down to the members; so if someone with a nasty spirit is leading you, you are more susceptible to receive that spirit. It became even more real when female ministry leaders blatantly voiced their attraction for me. I would always respond by saying "no, I'm not like that. You are a nice person, but I'm not into women". One particular woman's response was, "You're not like that now, but you will be—I'm going to pray about that". That's a shame! You know that you're doing something wrong, but because you want someone else to partake with you so badly, you pray for their demise—I should have dipped out of that church that very day and never returned. But me being me, I shrugged the comment off and figured the sistah was out of her mind because I just knew that sexing another woman was not going to happen with me.

C)   Be careful of what you let somebody speak in your life—or even what you speak over your own life—because, I guess, that lady really did pray for or wish for me to be attracted to women, just didn't end up being her. And then it happened. The "baby" was born. It was literally as if I woke up one morning and was attracted to a young lady. Honestly, I had no attraction to other women, just one in particular. She was a part of the church family as well. I remembered speaking to her on several occasions and she seemed to be pretty nice. I do remember saying to myself that she looked interesting [she was my first encounter with a lesbian "stud"], and that I would have liked to get to know her better. Over time, my relationship with the stud began to progress and my attraction and curiosity grew. I knew in my soul that this was wrong and needed some help with understanding why I was experiencing those feelings. I knew that the temptation was presented, and no entity had enough power over me to make me do it— so I couldn't blame devil. I was working on getting myself together, but my flesh was still weak. My "little girl" still had too much say so. So one day, I went to talk to my pastor about the situation because I just was not comfortable with the whole idea of being attracted to a chick—I loved men. I went in to the pastor's study and we began to chat. Before I could get my whole story out about why I asked for the meeting, he pretty much knew what I was going through, so he finished my thought/speech for me. His answer to my dilemma was "I believe that people can be born gay" and proceeded to say that it was pretty much okay and normal for me to feel the feelings that I felt. Aw, hell naw! I knew he was telling me the wrong crap. That was like saying, "God you made a mistake...I was really supposed to be a man, but you made me a woman," or vice versa. Not long after that, I finally left the church. I had received all of the spiritual erosion and corruption that I could take.

The stud and I dated for about two and a half to three years. She treated me better than any of the men I ran into ever did and really showed me how, as a man's woman, I want to be and should be treated in any future relationship(s). If she exists, then I know for definite that there is a man out there for me, who will supersede her efforts. During my relationship with the young lady, there were times when I would just break down because of guilt, but she really understood and knew that it was a spiritual battle that I had going on and tried her best to console me. She was more so like a best friend than a girl friend—but the difference was that we were sexually active with each other. Though the sex was quite pleasing, I missed men—the touch, the feel, and the overall experience.

As with most homosexual relationships, we had our share of drama, but it was nowhere near as much as in other homosexual relationships that I've witnessed. After the one and only time that we actually had a physical altercation, I knew then that I wouldn't be able to do that relationship much longer. I'm not with all that drama, fighting, and arguing, no ma'am and no sir; I'm not going to be able to do all of that. Too much estrogen or too much testosterone in an intimate relationship doesn't seem like it would produce lasting results. Just like yellow and blue make green, men and women compliment each other and create a balanced union. The two separate species both have great value to add to a relationship, and the difference in views and opinions helps us to grow and open our minds to different perspectives.

The young lady and I had so many more good moments than bad, but I knew that our relationship was not supposed to be and would not last. I do recall a time that she asked me to marry her, but despite the fact that I didn't want to hurt her,

I didn't (and still don't) do the gay marriage thing. Letting go of what seemed to be a good thing was not really what I wanted to do, but I knew that it had to be done. I remember telling her that I loved and truly cared for her, but that I could never give her what she was seeking and though it hurt at that moment, I had to end our relationship. I wanted her to be with someone who she could share her good heart with and someone who would freely love her, preferably a man, but if a woman was/is who she wanted, I still hoped that she found someone who would be good to her, just as she was to me. She understood, there was no harshness between the two of us, and plus, I still cared about her well-being and just about her as a person. Once that relationship was over, I knew that I would never date a chick again because I could not deal with the guilt or the drama.

After ending that relationship, I had sexual trysts with three other girls. I preferred the "studs" or dominant types because they more closely resembled boys. I guess that was a psychological thing. I felt convicted by the act, but because the women seemed masculine, in my mind, it lessened the severity of it.

Though I had great orgasms, the sex was meaningless and empty, and that's all it would be because these were encounters, interactions, and relationships built solely upon lust.   I continued on in "the life" for another year or less and finally made the decision to let it go.   I had been away from men for too long. Time and the real, not a strap-on, penis was calling me back to the heterosexual side.

Resolution of the Climax

Just as during an orgasm, when you're riding the wave of pleasure it may feel cataclysmically good, but it doesn't last forever. There's only so much you can take before you have to come down from the momentary high, thus entering the resolution phase of the climax.

Shortly after making the decision to walk away from the whole lesbian scene, I began to meet men again. I began to feel the desire to be in a relationship with a man and possibly work toward marriage at some point. This was a first for me because I usually saw men as objects of lust and partners to help fulfill the level of satisfaction that I was seeking. I guess I viewed men in the same way that some of them view women—as a piece of—well you know what I mean. I wanted a little more this time around. I had some ideas of what the prototype would be, but didn't have a clue as to how we would find each other.

The first guy that I met and got involved with seemed pretty cool initially, but only time would prove what he was made of. We hung out almost everyday, talked on the phone often and had sex a few, maybe three, times. He seemed to enjoy my company a lot, but for some reason, he got on my nerves. I thought that maybe it was because, when it came to men, I was used to being by myself—just sexing them, not dating any of them. It was all right that we hung out, I just didn't have to see him everyday and I didn't need to converse with him on a daily basis either. From the way it sounds, I think I was just physically attracted to him; and as far as the sex was concerned, he was the kinkiest of all the men I had encounters with. Though he gave me extensive hours of pleasure, was willing to try almost anything, and put forth his best effort to please me, I never achieved orgasm. I guess I wasn't as in to him.

Often times he would suggest that we were in an exclusive relationship, and as much as I wanted to be in a dating relationship with a man, he just wasn't where it was. I couldn't agree to that. He seemed to get upset because I disagreed with the idea of us being together. I just wasn't feeling him like that. It was just something about him that didn't feel right to me. After about two and a half to three months of carrying on, our relationship ceased to exist because I found out first hand/the hard way that he was a career criminal, looking for the next opportunity. I guess I was supposed to be the opportunity, but Jesus had to be really looking out for me because the majority of his plans and schemes for me did not prosper. I had to let go of him and that whole messed up situation because letting my vagina lead me almost landed me in jail on voluntary manslaughter or murder charges. Though that didn't turn out the way that I wanted it to, I attempted to hold on to the notion that, if at first you don't succeed, you got to try again.

After my relationship with that guy, I decided to go back to reconcile my relationship with the Lord. After I left that "gay church", my going to church services slacked up because it just left a bad taste in my mouth. I couldn't fathom going to another church where all those extra-curricular activities were going on. I didn't want to go to another church service just because it was Sunday or just because it was a Tuesday or Wednesday night Bible study. I wanted to go and find some real Jesus and I was really skeptical about where to get Him. I couldn't have my soul being played with and tainted like that again. While out of church, I did my share of things that I knew were not pleasing in God's eyes, but I just felt like I was doing me—being the person who I was created to be. I still had morals and beliefs, but I think that some times I chose to lay those aside and block out the conscience that I did have because I, often times, felt that life gave me nothing but bull crap. Once I regained my senses and remembered the foundation that my life was built upon, I knew that no one else, especially not I, could clean up the mess of my life that I had made, only God could.

After getting back into church, I was trying to get myself, and my life together for peace sake. I would faithfully go and receive the Word and felt it was really helping me. I believe that maybe four or five months went by and I had no sexual activity, and I didn't have a sex buddy in the picture, so I felt that I was doing well—though I was getting a little weak.

During those four to five months, I did end up meeting a guy at a cookout. I recalled seeing him on several pictures at my friend's house, thinking that he looked familiar, but never realizing why. As soon as I walked into the door at this party, he seemed to be the first person I saw. I diverted my glances from his direction and spoke to everyone as I entered, reminding myself that my intentions were harmless for that night. I just was out kicking it with my homegyrls, not trying to let my "little girl" take over. For the most part, we all just sat around chatting, socially drinking, and really getting our eat on. Most of the men had migrated outside to the patio and the ladies were inside doing what we do—mostly engaging in girl talk. Eventually, the guy from the photo came back into the house and decided that he wanted to sit right next to me, but before he sat down, I had to peep him out since he was up close. Right away, I noticed that he had on a nice amount of blue, from the hat on his head to the soles of his shoes. Automatically, I thought, "he must be gang affiliated", but attempting to not be judgmental, I didn't want to make assumptions. And as soon as he sat in the chair, I recognized why he looked so familiar. It had to have been at least fifteen years or so since the last time I had seen him, and actually, I didn't know him, I knew his sister. I knew of him, but back in our elementary school days, he and I never would have been mistaken as friends—we were two totally different people with, seemingly, nothing in common. After striking up conversation and gaining some sort of rapport with him, I asked about the blue, and sure enough, he was a banger. He said he lived in California and would come to Memphis often to visit family. We talked for a while and then he left, but before he came back to the party, my friends and I had already dipped out. I enjoyed our conversation and knew that, though our encounter was brief, we would meet again.

It may have been shortly before or shortly after meeting Mr. Cali that I met someone else, but knew that my attraction to him was and would be totally different than what it usually was with other guys. I knew of this guy, but never knew him personally, and honestly, wasn't even sure how and why I noticed him at that point. It's almost as if he just stood out more than the rest. There was some form of attraction resonating inside of me for him, slightly lustful, but more harmless. It was as if I really wanted to befriend him—and felt that we would really be good friends if given the opportunity to get to know one another. I would always say hello when I would see him in passing, he'd smile and quoted the usual, "Hey, how you doing?," and we'd continue on going our separate ways—but within me, I smiled because I knew that one day, he would know me and that we'd be friends. But at that moment, my "little girl" wanted to befriend someone as well, and at that time, he wasn't the one she was focused on.

It had to have been a month after meeting Mr. Cali that I received a phone call from a strange, long-distance number that I didn't know. When I answered, a male voice with a west coast dialect was on the other end asking to speak with me. Slightly perplexed about how he got my number, I proceeded to carry on a conversation with him. We chatted for a quick minute and Mr. Cali and I decided that we would connect and hang within the next few days. Conversations with him were very interesting and thorough. Once we began hanging out, most of our time was spent chatting the hours away—allowing each other the freedom to be ourselves. I was feeling him a little, but knew that our interaction was based on lustful attractions, and the "little girl's" main goal was to become acquainted with his "little man". Needless to say, they met, became good friends, and hung out with each other on several occasions until the day that they both got so caught up that conception occurred.

Things changed drastically! The cool friend that I thought I knew became an A-hole from hell. Mr. Cali really attempted to treat me like I was just some random whore on the streets. He knew that he was the only one that I was sexually involved with at that time, but had enough gall to say that the child wasn't his. He offered to pay for an abortion several times, telling me that if I didn't get one, I was opting to have a fatherless child. Even going so far as to say that if and when he makes it big, I better not try to contact him or put him on child support. That was just the last straw for me--yet, producing another situation that could have been potentially fatal because I allowed the vagina to lead me. It amazed me how he felt that he would be a successful somebody and I would be nothing. After hearing all of that nonsense, I wanted nothing to do with him and made a vow to God that I would do my best raising the child, even if I had to go at it alone. I did want a child, but the conditions just were not what I preferred. I've never wanted a "baby's daddy". I've always wanted for my husband and me to raise our children together; and that is why I thank God to this very day that I had a miscarriage a month after finding out that I was pregnant. Hallelujah!

Once Mr. Cali found out about the miscarriage, he implied that he wanted to continue our "friendship" as if nothing ever happened. He couldn't be serious. Shortly after all of this went down, he returned to California, and we didn't speak anymore. Months later, he called me several times, but I never was "available" to answer the phone. He surprised me almost two years later when, out of the clear blue sky, he showed up at my parents' house looking for me. He said something about trying to contact me, but never could reach me. I was nice enough to give him a few minutes of conversation. I try hard not to do the "grudge thing", but that surely doesn't mean that you will get a second try at messing me over. Mr. Cali even had the audacity to, straight out, ask for sex. At that point, I had been without any sex for well over a year. I told him that straight forward, but he wasn't trying to hear it. So I guess I had to make it even plainer. I explained that there was no way in the world that he should've expected anything from me after the episode that occurred between us—which he referred to it as "a little incident that we almost had". Foolishness! I guess I told him what he didn't want to hear. He tried a few more times to get into the panties, not realizing that I was so very serious about him not standing a chance. I really couldn't understand what made him feel like he deserved anything from me, especially sex, after what I experienced with him. I guess he finally got the picture because I never heard from him again.

Prior to the, almost, two year later appearance, I started picking up the pieces, got a new job and reverted back to my attempts at being celibate. I think I may have met a few guys here and there, but nothing ever progressed beyond flirt sessions. I made up my mind that I was not looking for another sex buddy. I was looking for a friend, maybe with the potential of growing into more. At the job site where I was working at the time, there were so many more men working for the company than women, but I was not attracted to most of them and the majority of them were married—and that was a line that I vowed to never cross. I've never been fond of breaking up homes.

Four months had passed since the last time I had partaken in any sexual activities. I seemed to be maintaining pretty well because, usually, by my fourth month of going without, I would really have a strong yearning to please and be pleased. Church seemed to have been helping, yet at that point I wasn't as focused on trying not to have sex, I just was more choosy about to whom I wanted to give it.

I can recall one particular day at the office when there was a guy who walked in that I didn't recall seeing before. I spoke with him a time or two when he would phone in to the job, but I'd never seen him in person. Over the phone, he seemed really short-tempered and attitudinal. So meeting him wasn't really on my "to-do" list. While in the office, one of the ladies who worked at the company whispered to me that he was so sexy. I figured I'd look to see who she saw because I, obviously, wasn't paying any attention. When I turned around, to my surprise, he was a handsome, chocolate brother. I may have said hi, but I think I left it at that because I was trying to stay focused on my celibacy. At some point, I caught his eye and he caught mine. No words were exchanged, but a conversation was surely taking place. He just seemed to ooze sex appeal and within a moment's time, I created a whole scene of possibilities within my head. I quickly tried to push out the thoughts because I figured that he might have been married since most of the other men I encountered at this company were already taken.

A few weeks or so passed and I got him on my telephone extension one day. Before he knew it, he slipped and made a comment that confirmed his interest. I just laughed it off and tried to maintain as much professionalism as possible. Then, the day came when playing nice was out the window and getting down to the nitty gritty was what he had in mind. In a casual conversation, he asked if he could take me out and I said okay because I didn't see a problem with that. I inquired about what we'd do, but he said he'd leave it up to me. Thinking to myself and speaking it aloud before I could find better words to say, "I'm not sure if leaving it up to me is what you want to do. You don't know what I'm capable of." He laughed and in so many words, I just told him that I'd leave it up to him, but his response was very similar to mine. Seemingly, we both had the same agenda. We made our arrangements and just before releasing the line, he posed the question, "You do know that I'm married, right?" No I didn't know, but I knew that what I said after I told him no shouldn't have been said—but it was the truth [still was wrong though]. I explained to him how, normally, I didn't (and still don't) practice getting involved in anyone's marriage simply because I view marriage as a sacred union, but instead of thinking with my morals and spirit, I was thinking with my sex.

We engaged in sex twice, but I knew that it just wasn't right at all. Based on the sexual experiences that I had before him, including the sex with the females, the experience with him, overall, was so much better. Usually, when you encounter great sex, you can't get enough, but in my case, this was a problem...reminds me of that blues song that says it seems so much better or feels so good when you're stealing it. It just wasn't right. The sex we had should not have been as intense and pleasurable as it was because of the fact that he was married—I was just outside cat. I had already stepped outside of my moral boundaries and I knew that if I kept sexing him, it would only produce chaotic and problematic results. I couldn't continue on being hypocritical. I couldn't continue violating his marriage like that because I do want to be married one day and I wouldn't want to be in that same situation as his wife—thinking that everything is all good, but my husband is out there laid up in somebody's mouth, vagina, anus, or something. I was just not going to be able to continue on.

At the time, I had a married friend-girl who would always say to me that "if he ain't worried about his wife, why should you?" My response would be something to the effect of "because his wife is a person who doesn't deserve to be lied to, cheated on, and messed over". I'm not saying that I'm a saint; I just value the "Golden Rule", no matter how dead or meaningless it may seem to be in our society. Not saying that it's easy to always treat people the way you want to be treated—especially when some make dealing with them so difficult—but I figure it's worth a try. Though my desire for Mr. Chocolate was strong [I promise that it was strong], my desire to do the right thing was even stronger. I figured that, if I had been in church all of my life and was claiming to know God, Jesus and the Holy Spirit, at some point I needed to reflect it.

This may sound crazy to some, but honestly, from the situation with Mr. Chocolate, my desire to be married heightened. Yes, we were both wrong, but we didn't have to stay in the wrong, continuing to indulge in it. I had a choice to make, and I chose to not keep interfering with their promise. My initial motivation for this choice was my thinking that if the sex was this good and passionate with him and he belonged to someone else, how much better would it be if I was doing it in the right relationship—with the man that I belonged to and he belonged to me? Needless to say, I started back on my journey to celibacy and since then, have been a whole lot more successful at it.

The Last Drop

Do you recall the dude (referenced as Mr. Dude) I mentioned earlier, who I met during or before the time that I met Mr. Cali? I knew in my soul that we would be good friends and for the last few years, we have been. I can proudly admit that no sex has taken place—that was such a small part of my overall attraction to him and desire to get to know him. A nice portion of the men that I had met and befriended were the ones I engaged in sex with, at least once. While attempting to go without sex on the previous occasions, I would end up meeting a guy who I was attracted to, and we'd commit the act, but the relationship was empty. So with Mr. Dude, I've seen my own level of growth and self-control. I give myself a pat on the back for taking control of the "little girl" and not allowing her to run me. There is so much more to people than sex. When we just take a moment to get to know someone without playing a role, telling lies, or saying all the right things just to taste, feel, touch, and experience the package in between their legs, we gain an opportunity to learn so much. In taking the time to dig deeper and get to know someone, we could possibly create lasting relationships that would have otherwise been ruined by a sexual encounter. It's a sad case when the only thing others know about you is your ability/inability to perform sexually. Sex can only take you so far, and when the drive or ability to perform declines, on what do you have to fall back? For those of us with the nymphomaniac nature, sometimes it's worth sacrificing that momentary release to explore the endless possibilities that come with forming relationships with substance.

In an effort to sum up this conversation with you, or monologue since I'm not able to hear your responses, I want to say that despite what you have been told or led to believe, sex is more than just a three letter word. It is more than just a manifestation of lust; more than an act of passion; more than a method of reproduction; more than a good marketing tool. It is more than a way to build an empty or false ego; more than any form of pornography; more than a crime of power and passion; and more than just an avenue for orgasm. Just know that it's so much more than what we limit it to be. It wasn't created to be a detestable, life-threatening act, but a life forming, beautiful expression of love, desire, passion, and intimacy.

No Greater Love; the Dedication

by GT

You give me paradise on earth that no one can take
away
Please forgive me for the times that I allowed
Circumstances to make my feelings sway.
As Beyonce' said, You love me "flaws and all"
That's why whenever I need anything; it's You who I
always call.
I must be crazy to allow my mind to give way to
doubt
Because I know for a fact that even when I get on
Your last nerves
You still come through to help me out.
I'm sorry for the times that I allowed others to
interfere and I pushed
You to the side, foolishly walking away from Your
amazing love that You never tried to hide.
Thinking I'd find better love elsewhere,
You allowed me to venture out on my own
While You sat back patiently waiting for the day I'd
come back home.

You knew the grass wasn't greener on the other side

and that only You could love me best, so now that

I've realized the truth and came back home, You're

putting my love to the test.

Though my suffering sometimes hurt both you and

me, I do understand your reasons why,

You want to make sure that no one or no thing will

ever make me leave again,

no matter how hard they try

Though temptation may get strong, I know what's

real—

You give amazing love—not the kind that hurts but

the kind that heals

No one can ever do what You do; I found that out the

hard way,

That's why my love for You and this relationship

Grows stronger each and every day.

To God

Reader Reviews/Comments

Great technique—using a comical approach to tackle a sensitive subject. The novel was great. I was intrigued, hungry for more, and enjoyed the colorful pictures created using words. I also enjoyed the in depth discussion, and the comparison between flesh and spirit. The poetry was pure icing on the cake.
 Y. Bell

Very creative writer. Such an animated speaker. This novel is needed because the subject affects us all. People need someone to speak openly about this taboo and sensitive subject that is so often swept under the rug.
 J. Mosby

Creative usage of words. I admire the honesty. Very interesting and enlightening read.
T. Bradley.

I like the concept of bringing a taboo issue, straight to your face. I like the way this book opens your eyes to something people would rather overlook or pretend is not happening as much as they think.
J'son W.

This book was refreshing and candid. It expressed a lot of things that we wonder but are not willing to verbalize. People sometimes shy away from their sexuality and I think this is worth a read!
 Minister C. Blake

www.ingramcontent.com/pod-product-compliance
Lightning Source LLC
Chambersburg PA
CBHW031327040426
42443CB00005B/240